IT'S TOMORROW SOMEWHERE

poems by e.jinjin

Copyright © 2021 e.jinjin
All rights reserved.
Cover art by Danae Wilson
Proofread by Jonah Branding & Emily Jensen
ISBN: 978-0-578-90796-3

Shout Outs

Mariah & Sydney
Will & Theda
Ashley & Jonah
Katie & Emily
Marlowe & Chanel
Juztis & Kyle

Contents

Dark as a Dream ... 9

The Color of Leaving ... 39

It's Only Rain ... 69

Growth (Or Lack Thereof) ... 99

Dark As A Dream

Dahlia

This is a story about a woman named Dahlia. She loved dogwood flowers, pasta puttanesca, and her yellow rain boots.

Her tired hands cross stitched the screen of the back door and pressed all the little knots tight with her pinky nail. Precision was crucial.

She whispered signs backwards as she drove past them [*thgir nrut tsum enal thgir*] hexing herself and the asphalt she drove over.

Sometimes she just wanted to get out of her skin. She felt like it was suffocating her. Everything was so goddamn itchy all the time.

Her therapist said she might try to write. But writing about your own melancholia can be hard, so she wrote about Dahlia instead.

Remembering

Remembering the time you told me when you fell in love with me / how the warmth slid through the morning blinds like a deck of cards / sunlight spades on my neck / and you watched me breathe / shallow / lost in a dream of you / please don't let me forget this one

I can't remember all the fights / all the times I cried until I couldn't speak / all the times you held me tight like a prayer / I can't remember the paths you traced along the length of my spine / your fingers like warm sugar / or the way it felt to be pressed together like two sides of a zipper / but I remember I loved you

But the memories are unremembering / was your hair short or long / was my fingernail polish chipped at the edges like crumpled cellophane / were we sick to our stomachs from the milkshakes the night before / did we lose it all the same way we found it in the first place / I wish I could remember everything the right way / and I wish it didn't have to hurt

The Ticket Collector

you're the ticket collector at the entrance of every dream / but I think you fell asleep in a corner of my memory / sometimes your snoring wakes me up / what's the difference between almost and too real / salty skin cravings / fingertips / speak to me in spanish and electricity / wake me up again / mile high naps / smoking indoors / hands with secrets smeared like permanent marker / play with my hair / pull it like carnival taffy / nostalgia tickles my throat every time you almost wake up / my mind dreams dreams of your hands on my waist / how is it possible you are the one that got away and the one I never had

A Lesson In Conditional Clauses

What if the birds stopped killing themselves
Waiting for us to find their delicate bodies
Mangled underneath the sliding glass door

What if the Moon melted into a pool of mercury
A weightless liquid mirror split again and again
Until the sky looked like a fractured windshield

What if we could move time off its fragile axis
Stepping over sailing stones and around Viking ships
And hold every mistake we made in our palms

Preguntas y Respuestas

What street was it?
I was wearing a red dress.
The day before or after we laughed about birds?
Huevos en la cama, por fa.
It was dark.
Did you mean to?
Definitely the buses.
The string wouldn't untangle.
Bright pink or yellow?
I didn't see the car coming.
Do you remember?
Uno dos tres...cinco seis siete.
We couldn't have been too far from the hostel.
How much is that in pesos?
You didn't say goodbye.
Was it before I ate the tuna?
It was always 7.
Calle Independencia or Cinco de Mayo?
Just for a second and just fingertips.
Is it bad to wonder?
I do every day.

Teapot Genie

I made a home inside a teapot
Porcelain lacquered royal blue
Gold sunburst around the spout
You found it at a garage sale
Said it was sweet like me
The inside was quiet
Plain white walls decorated with
Invisible Rembrandt paintings
Dark as a dream with the lid on
I waited for the whistle for so long
I can't remember
Not waiting

Miss Heidi

Miss Heidi always wore a pale pink cotton leotard, pale pink nylon tights, and a flimsy pale pink wrap skirt. Her curly russet hair twisted up and around into her tortoise shell clip. Loose pieces and freckle constellations framed her face.

Arms forward. First position. Chins up.

Miss Heidi did a solo every year during the recital. One year she danced to *Ave Maria*. A single spotlight followed her cutting through the dark like butter. The audience held their breath in their fists. She slid across the stage. Her body was moonlight champagne.

Rond de jambe. Second position. Fingers light.

Miss Heidi's oatmeal leg warmers bunched at her ankles. Before leaving the studio, she would shed them like snakeskin and toss them into the basket of her bicycle before riding home. In the winter she wrapped a scarf tight to her neck and tottered off in a flurry of frosty meteorites.

Plié. Tension in your back. Power in your arms.

Miss Heidi lived in the white house with the red ivy-covered trellis on Main Street. Before bed she drank tea with her husband on the screened-in porch and watched the dusk lumber in. He held her face in his hands and kissed each freckle constellation trying to find his way home.

Port de bras. Lengthen your spine. Abs tight.

Miss Heidi had two daughters; one hundred forty-six and two sons if you counted her students. They clung to her pale pink leotard like the ivy on her trellis. She stayed until the last of them bustled out of the studio. They called her the North Star.

And grande plié. Perfect posture. Heads high.

Again.

Gas Station Gothic

Today I got gas
It was snowing
Heavy lazy flakes
Two landed on my eyelashes
I left my gloves on the passenger seat
The ones from his mom last Christmas
The guy at pump seven
Blue flannel and Carhartts
Caused a scene
His card was declined three times
The handle clicked twice
Drops of gasoline slid to the concrete
Mr. B taught us gasoline
Can never completely freeze
I pressed *NO* for the receipt

Genevieve

Genevieve forgave her son's disappearing act
And the subsequent cursing at his own funeral

His voice a thin gauze over the casket
White and translucent like the roses on his chest

Fuck him, he only ever cared about himself
She held his hand all the way to the car

Rinsed his hair with lukewarm peach schnapps
Diluting the oily rainbow in the parking lot

He ate fat green olives on the drive home
The tissue box jostled under the seat

His grenade mouth leaked mustard gas and jam
Genevieve held the silence like a crowbar

~~Lost &~~ Found & Lost

He pressed her hand like a flower
Bookended by that explosive fight about kids
They had in the desert in the spring
Maybe it would be enough
To preserve themselves
Curate a museum exhibit of
Bodies and tumbleweed and memories
Something people could come all over
To marvel at and stretch their arms
Past the No Touching signs
Wishing they had kept their lost things too

The Yellow Pitcher

Every Saturday we wandered through the market
with the high ceilings. Our fingers ran along rows
of dimpled oranges and glossy apples.

You were allowed one sample of saltwater taffy. I
always chose blue. You always chose pink and
red swirl. Traditions aren't meant to be broken.

Every Saturday my eyes lingered a little bit
longer on the yellow pitcher. I imagined it on our
kitchen table one day full of fresh cut flowers.

*You know you're allowed to treat yourself
sometimes, right?* You always teased. I lifted it
up to see the price tag underneath. $34.98.

Every Saturday I walk along the newly paved
trails to pick wildflowers for the yellow pitcher.
It's not on our kitchen table. It's on my dresser.

You haven't been to the market since February
when I dropped the yellow pitcher on accident.
The handle shattered noisily at my feet.

Heartbreak

sometimes heartbreak feels like saving the best part of a meal for the end and then getting there and realizing you're already kind of full / do you know the feeling of getting called on in class when you're not paying attention / or when you're in the middle of a dream and you begin falling and you wake up and you're shaking / sometimes it feels like my fault / okay / a lot of the time it feels like my fault / i know they say it takes two to tango / but i really feel like i'm leading / do you think bomb technicians ever feel like doll makers / do they enjoy the intimacy they have with all those tiny wires and fine details before the explosion / i wish i could scoop up the mushroom cloud and put it in a little tupperware at the very back of the fridge / would things have been better if it hadn't been him / probably / do you know the feeling of getting called on in class when you're not paying attention and then it turns out you're not even in the right classroom / or when you're in the middle of a dream and you begin falling but your body won't wake up / my fingertips smell like sulfur and destruction / i can't find my heart

Almost Wedding

A parcel of white lace floating into honeyed
lovehalls of candied violins and champagne

Three pearl buttons and a diamond and four
brown eyes waiting whispering two panicking

Teeth sparkling stretching dental floss telephone
wires between snowflake earrings hanging by a nerve

Remembered dreams sliding off an origami veil like
cake frosting if this is forever I don't think we should

What We Can't Talk About

Driving home from dance class on Tuesday in
the minivan with the squeaky brakes

DW's seat belt doesn't go through the loop of the
hand-me-down booster seat

Just the Way You Are humming through the
dashboard courtesy of Star 105.7

Mom's dinner plate eyes sweeping his side of the
garage where the white Impala used to be

The yellow sticky note on the white door like a
pat of butter on a pile of mashed potatoes

Her hands forgetting what to do and dropping
her purse in the dust and oil on the cement floor

Footsteps on carpet on hardwood echoing
through the house over and over and over

Walking past a Mom I didn't know looking too
small in a bed too big in a house too big

DW's observations and Mom searching for the
answers in a crumpled yellow sticky note

He took all his clothes, but he left all the hangers.

NIGHTTIME

This is when The Feelings begin their trapeze act

It wouldn't be so bad
        Up in the air
        Pinpricks against the spotlight
        Swinging on chalked palms
If The Feelings weren't so clumsy
        So eager to slip
        Never well-rehearsed
        Already braced for the crush of the net

The Stick-Up

Depression goes for a blowout at the salon
Paints bubblegum lips velvet with cyanide
Sprays her hair with venom from the asp that killed Cleopatra
One drop of White Flag perfume on custard wrists
a delicate blend of lilac, yuzu, and a wrinkled suicide note
She shimmies into her sexiest dress (the red one
responsible for the fact that vehicle occupant
death rates are 1.8 to 2.6 times higher for males than females)
And slides the handgun into the pocket sewn inside her leather jacket

Depression walks into the bank all fiery eyes and Coke bottle curves
At my teller window I squint because I know her from somewhere
but I can't remember where
The air around her smells familiar and intoxicating
She leans forward on the counter with one elbow and
unzips her jacket just enough for me to know she's armed
You have three seconds to give me everything you've got

Holy

We built church steeples out of vertebrae
Pretty in the dark I can still see your eyes
Inscrutable nocturnal every blink deliberate
The streetlight outside lulling us
To sleep with hazy rectangles on the walls
Playing the chords of a thousand hymns
Your thumb across my lips
A communion wafer pressed
Like a promise I wish you could keep

Louise

Louise is sixty-two years old and her body is
softer than it used to be. She lives with her
mother in the faded blue house she grew up in.
They steal cable from their next-door neighbor.

When she was sixteen her stained-glass hands
held a boy with curly hair and he wanted to know if
everything inside her was just as holy. His hips
asked questions she didn't know how to answer.

When she was sixteen she became a mother,
a receptionist, and a victim of her first broken
heart. Suspect: male, roughly 5'10", asparagus
eyes, laugh like her father's, hips without answers.

Louise is sixty-two years old, and she crouches in
the garden and gathers four tomatoes and two
green peppers in the folds of her apron. Last
year she watched her boyfriend die in the hallway.

Her niece is sixteen, and when she visits she
always wants Auntie Lou's famous salsa. Her
hands are stained from the vegetables and the
soil. *Auntie Lou, how do you know when you're in love?*

I don't know. I never have.

The Understudy

ACT ONE : SCENE ONE

Julie just got a manicure. Every perfect almond nail buffed and polished in her favorite shade of pink: *Scheming Bitch* by O.P.I.

It's his birthday and like any good understudy, she observes, takes mental notes, and hopes the lead will suddenly fall ill.

I watch her watch me, his arm thrown lazily around me, my hand resting lightly on his leg, my head on his shoulder.

He gets up to mix another drink. She jumps up to follow, to flirt for twenty minutes in the kitchen, to squeeze lime onto his tongue.

When he comes back, he slides in next to me, kisses my cheek. *Why don't you ever get your nails done like Julie?* She smiles.

END SCENE.

SHE SPIRALED

She laid on the floor
She thought of the man who had loved her
She thought of her friends
She thought of nothing
Her vision didn't cloud
She didn't see stars
She saw the line where the wall met the ceiling
She forgot what her face looked like
She saw the monotonous blinking of the smoke detector
She felt the rough carpet under her hands
She felt nothing

Ghost

She somersaults up the walls and pirouettes on the kitchen ceiling. On the tip of my nose she balances and does an arabesque like a sultry weathervane. She sits crisscross applesauce at the dinner table and waits for Dad to say *amen*. I am the only one that sees her foxtrot in the macaroni salad. *Aren't you hungry? Not anymore.*

Every night she writes a letter to the Moon using the inside of a spoon and one chopstick. The Moon never writes back. At night she sleeps beneath pools of wisteria with her eyes open. She teaches the bats how to chain smoke Virginia Slims in the treetops and the frogs how to deal cards on the lily pads. As the stars blink awake, her speakeasy is in full swing. I shut my window to muffle the din.

During the day she watches me work from inside the dusty computer screen. She opens funny emails and tries to make me laugh. I log off. Everyone keeps asking if I'm okay and I say I am. *We haven't seen her in a while. Do you know when she'll be coming back?*

Recurring Nightmare

He watches me naked in my crooked sleep
I dream again of a wildfire I can't escape
Parties I'm not invited to
Sweet nicotine tangerine lips
My popcorn nerves burn me alive
I'm falling and I wake up in his arms
I'm right here. You're safe.

Smoke

I. Vettia held her newborn son tight against the fabric of her stola. He coughed and writhed like the beetle she saw climbing along the edge of the fountain yesterday morning. Little fingers grasping nothing. Eyes red from the heat. Balsam and cinnamon breath hot. Shallow. Weak. Her tears fell on his cheeks as she watched the smoke rise above the cypress trees like a grumbling angry fog. The ochre and mollusk tint on her lips ran hot and wet down the corners of her mouth. Smoke and ash slid down her throat as she watched her son grow limp. Her parchment bones were found in April 1748 under the weight of Mount Vesuvius' deposits. Frozen like a beetle in amber. The man who found her wondered if she had been beautiful.

Build a story out of smoke. Of love. Of loss. Make it real. Make it hurt. Make them wonder if anyone can ever run.

II. This was the time Shelby taught me how to make a bowl out of a plastic water bottle we found in the trash. It was dark in Alena's house and I think Andrea was taking a shit out on the deck into the river. *Lay the aluminum foil flat. Like this.* We used our fingers to seal the edges. She pulled her hair back into a messy ponytail and took out one of her earrings. *Poke holes in it.* I don't know why all the lights were off in the house. Alena's mom forgot to put the leftovers away in the fridge again. I could hear Andrea calling for toilet paper. We took our shirts off so our moms couldn't smell it on us. The stars floating on the silver river made it feel like we were at a disco. *Now inhale. Again.*

Remind them what it's like to fill your pretty lungs with angst. The sour taste of your Mom's disappointment.

III. Frida Kahlo seduced the woman her husband cheated on her with. Frida waited for her lover to come home. She was never late and she adored that about her, along with her perfect Cinderella feet. Frida would let her bleed onto the canvas and tie her hair around the edges in sailor's knots. Her nightgown hung low. The neckline exposed tiny goosebumps all along her collarbone like flecks of paint. She struck a match against the sandpaper wall and lit a cigarette poised between her fingers. Before taking a drag, she examined herself in the mirror. She felt daring. Sexy. A little tipsy from the shot of mezcal she had earlier. The first exhale spilled from her lips as the door creaked open. *What took you so long?*

Teach them how cigarettes are made. How the thin bundled fibers of the filter are meant to prevent large amounts of smoke from being inhaled. How the chemicals are supposed to slow the burn. It's okay if it makes the smoke even sweeter.

IV. In 2013 Justin lit a cigarette with the rest of his buddies in Afghanistan. *Ruck up. We move tomorrow.* Gray halos hung over their heads as they laughed and swore and spit into the dusty earth. Sometimes he felt like they were on Mars. He sure as hell felt like an alien a lot of the time. His wife had just given birth to their second son. She named him Joseph after his grandfather. Justin missed the first birth too. Preston blew a thick wall into his face. *Get out of your head.* In two hours' time, an AR-15 will rip a hole through Justin's right femur. He will receive a Purple Heart and PTSD flashbacks for the rest of his life.

Remember when he came home and tore apart the living room trying to save us from IEDs under the sofa cushions? His wild eyes when he found an old Cheeto and a nickel.

V. I told Riley about the heart I was breaking. My hands counted money slower than normal. *One hundred. Two. And three hundred.* Positive my drawer wouldn't balance by 5. Positive I wouldn't make it to 5. She got me a bottle of water from the break room. Told me to sit. To take deep breaths. To think about what I was going to say. *I have to tell him. It's going to be horrible.* I chipped off the rest of my nail polish. Red flakes like blood on the black swivel chair fabric. My eyes were puffy. I cried twice in the bathroom before the first hour of my shift was up. *I've got smokes in my car. I've been trying to quit. Want the rest of 'em?*

Tell me, was it worth it?

Anxiety Metaphors I

The pull of gravity dryironing a stutter into the back of my throat

nobodylovesmenobodywantsmeiamalone

Candles slipslopping wax on the inside of my temples

Moving really fast in slow-motion and or moving really slow in fast-motion

Someone stuck a chute in me filled me with cement zipped me back up

I am an actress and my role today is Regular Person

I am not a very good actress

It's Getting Bad Again

And I don't really know how to stop it when it happens
The sun set at 6:52 today and I wore a sweatshirt under my coat
If I cut my hair, it won't matter because it will all grow back
Sometimes I think my breathing is weightless and I worry that people can tell
Dad and I used to have The Longest French Fry competitions at McDonald's
One time I picked up a French fry not knowing it was our last match
I don't like going for walks when it's so windy outside
Two years ago, I was in a car crash and my boyfriend picked glass out of my hair into the sink
Last week the sun set at 7:06 and I wore a fleece jacket
If I go away, it won't matter because everything will grow back

JOSHUA TREE
For Marlowe

I went away and I didn't come back / I mean I did / but not really / I left the small parts in the desert / the parts that crunched easily underfoot like frozen pipe cleaners / and I brought back some rocks / ones that sparkle if you hold them just right under the light / kind of like the toenail Moon / you always told me California was special / I didn't believe you at first / but you were right / it let me swap out old memories for new ones / that way I didn't really have to go back / at least / not all of me

Evening Walk

Standing by the headstone between
Two tall bushes on the ledge
There are clusters of
Pearly lily pads resting atop
The brown lake not too far below
Like stucco on glass but
The dead leaves everywhere make
It a difficult trek downward
Across the lake is a narrow path and
A small bridge and
A spot where two figures are fishing and
I wonder how they got over there
Because it looks much prettier than here
Was it a left or a right at the old church turned
Library now boarded up with
A lump of dirt in the parking lot?
And I realize it's the same dull path I took
To get to the headstone between
Two tall bushes on the ledge

The Color Of Leaving

Wellness Check-Up

Good, thanks. Yeah, I've been doing a lot better actually.
Okay.
Medium.
Medium.
Only sometimes.
High.
Never.
Medium? I don't know. I never really think about that.
High.
A few times a week probably.
Work is fine.
I've been trying to get outside more.
Yeah, I think it's helping.
10 mg a day.
I guess I would say 30 percent.
Only when it gets bad.
I know I should schedule a session. I keep forgetting.
Not too much anymore. Thank God.
Yeah.
It's like being on the edge of the Grand Canyon, but I'm not afraid of heights or falling.
I don't know.
I think I'm afraid I'll jump.

DIVINATION

A little girl in muddy sneakers gathers flower
petals and clusters of bark and pine needles and
mixes them up in the sand box until her mom
calls and says that the rest of the potion will
have to wait for tomorrow since it's getting dark

In high school she does her makeup in the gym
locker room before the bell and watches all the
Harry Potter movies at sleepovers with her
friends while they drink tea and try to translate the
dead shapes written at the bottom of their cups

She's lost her baby fat and college wraps her up
like an old cardigan and she lets the boy with the
glasses run the tips of his fingers over the
grooves worn into her palms letting the future
divine itself

Her twenties twist around love lost and mistakes
re-remembering themselves and she gives thanks
to the orange bottles standing watch like stoic
plastic gods waiting for an offering on her nightstand

Sadism

I made him read my poems
about the ones who weren't him

Helium Shortage

The world is running out of helium. The men and women who descend into the depths beneath the crusty shell of the Earth to harvest the gas with tool belts full of pumps and balloons in dozens of colors and shapes and sizes are now out of a job.

Six of them work out a trip with each other and their unemployment checks and their paid time off to Cappadocia, Turkey. Hundreds of balloons set sail every morning. The dull rainbow bulbs around their waists can't even begin to compare.

On Thursday, the six helium farmers cluster together with their colorful tool belts into a giant's wicker picnic basket. The flame hisses as they watch the rocky moonscape grow smaller and smaller. None of them have ever flown before.

All the time they spent underneath the Earth's surface they felt the crushing weight of gravity bouncing like flashlight beams off their bright yellow helmets. It never occurred to any of them that they might be afraid of heights.

June

June had a penchant for
Wicker furniture and orange groves
Even though she thought
The chairs uncomfortable
And oranges slimy
She curled up on the soft cushions
Of the sofa with an apple in her hand
And thought maybe in her next life
She would be better at loving
The things she loved

Brave Little Astronauts

In the 1990s, NASA sent thousands of jellyfish into outer space for a science experiment. The study was called "The Effects of Microgravity-Induced Weightlessness on Aurelia Ephyra Differentiation and Statolith Synthesis." Once acclimated to their new home, the jellies began to reproduce. By the end of the mission, more than 60,000 jellyfish orbited the Earth like translucent Easter eggs.

Take a baby from China and raise her by a white family in rural Michigan. It's a social experiment, really. How well will she do growing up the only minority? In what ways will she adapt? In what ways will she falter? To what degree will she deflect the blame of her shortcomings on her parents' ignorance and refusal to grow? What will she think of the woman who gave her up?

The little girl with bao bun cheeks will want to dye her hair blonde because that's how all her friends look. She'll crack a racist joke before anyone else thinking it better to have them laughing *with* her rather than *at* her. When she gets older, all her boyfriends will be white. She will try her best to slip through the cracks, which will work well for the most part until she realizes she exists in a cultural purgatory. A no man's land.

When the jellyfish returned to Earth, those born and raised in space didn't fully develop their sense of gravity. Up and down got all tangled. They had trouble getting around and often pulsated abnormally. The brave little astronauts had vertigo.

To The Handsome Stranger With The Dog Named Suitcase

I thought you were really sweet
When Suitcase dragged you up to my table on the patio
He was just a puppy but you could tell by his clumsy paws
that he'll be big one day
You apologized and flashed a smile
that made my insides all wobbly
When Suitcase planted himself right next to me
ate a bite of my sandwich
and gave me a big kiss
You asked what I was doing later not knowing
My flight left in an hour

Nathalie On Friday

The young man sat on the concrete to the east side of the post office every day. Sometimes he was in a wheelchair. She was told to always walk on the opposite side of the street. But the sidewalk near the post office had flower shapes carved into it. The grooves became spidery rivers during the rainy season. *Ten cuidado, mi cielo.*

On the last Thursday she crossed the street. Rainy season was drying up. Tourists would begin to arrive soon with their pale legs and bad accents. She bought a slice of torta chilena to eat in the park on her way home. The pigeons dawdled nearby keeping a close eye out for any stray crumbs. She cut the dessert into small pieces, placed the open plastic container on the edge of the park bench and walked home. The pigeons feasted.

Gone Fishin'

I caught a fish and he smiled
Told me seeing the sky
On the other side of the looking glass
Knocked the wind out of him
He described colors
I could only imagine
Like the color of the number 4
The color of trees laughing
The color of singing in the shower
I begged him to stay
Offered to build him a home
A nice tank near the kitchen window
He showed me the color of leaving

A Lesson In Phantom Limb Pain

The first night we drove to the dam
That song played on the car radio
As I jumped into the river
You followed me
First with your eyes
Then with your feet on the rocks
We smoked Black & Milds
In front of the capitol
And laughed in our underwear
Under a mosquito bite sky
Curfew was at midnight but it was already 3
Your hands were smooth
And I liked that you asked permission
That song stopped playing a year ago
Sometimes I catch myself still singing it
Expecting you to chime in at the chorus

HAPPY BIRTHDAY TO ME

this is not where i thought i would be
james dean died at 24 in a car accident
he was driving a porsche
can you see the age in my hands yet
you know the way old women's hands look
rice paper doorknobs
today i found a big yellow leaf
and dad left a note on my car
last year you took me out to dinner
where you wanted to go
and i paid the bill
i am getting better now
all on my own

Atlas

Maybe Atlas wasn't a powerful titan
Maybe he was just a metaphor for skeletons
Maybe supporting the heavens was a Sisyphean condemnation even for someone of his stature
Maybe his shoulders hurt just like ours
Maybe he knew no one was meant to endure eternity

The Mad Hatter Doesn't Drink Tea Anymore
For Jonah

On a very hazy evening he and Alice trip tipped
over thimbles and thumbles all the way to the
inside out school where they slipped glasses and
plates and spoons and sporks into their pockets

They laughed all the way to the jelly jam tree
near the bed of hazel eyed Susans where only a
whisper could travel and they dug up tissue
paper ice cubes for their gin and tonics

The Mad Hatter kept the gin in the first dresser
drawer next to the socks and knacks and knicks
and he and Alice trapped their giggles in firefly
jars so the White Rabbit wouldn't hear them

That hazy evening was at least two miles away
from Alice and now he was scrim scrambling
without shoes atop foggy crumbled cookie peaks
whose edges were trimmed with playing cards

But even so, no matter the distance, she liked
remembering the Hatter's laugh and the way
his fingers snapped confetti and they both knew
that eventually they'd find ways to fight
jabberwockies together again

Waking Up Anxious

There are butterfly knives in my veins
Tropical heat trapped in my jaw
Please tell me it can all be over soon

Proof

Icarus held each apparatus up to the light coming in from the window
They were weightless like paper dolls
He examined each bend and fold of the wings as though they were glass slides under a microscope
One of these would take him to the Sun

After five long minutes of excruciating indecision, he settled on a pair of two broad white wings
They resembled an albatross sunning itself on pebbles near the cove
He shimmied into them and tilted his neck from side to side to loosen up
Friday morning he was slated for takeoff

The Sun was watery and weak that fateful day
He licked his index finger and held it up to gauge the direction and intensity of the wind
His father shuffled awkwardly around his winged son and recited an unimpressive sailing metaphor
This is a mistake.
I know, but I have to make sure it is.
He was airborne at 6:47 a.m., and within five minutes had accumulated 12 bugs in his teeth

He circled around the bubbling Sun and squinted even behind the free sunglasses he got from his orthodontist's office
It was as beautiful and terrifying as he had imagined
Icarus didn't panic when his arm hair began to singe and the wax began to melt in great globs down his back
He had proven his hypothesis correct
He had made a mistake

STAN THE MOLE MAN COLLECTS CHANGE ON THE CORNER AND NOW HE'S ACROSS FROM ME ON THE SUBWAY WITH HIS HAND SOMEWHERE I'D RATHER NOT SAY SO I'LL PRETEND HE'S EATING SARDINES INSTEAD

His fat fingers barely fit
Under the rolled-up lid
Fingernails scraping
Against the tin
Disturbing the oil
Eyes scrunched up
Searching as if by echolocation
For that last slimy bit
Of the tail that broke off

Morning Poem

1. Wedge your fist in the hollow of the gasp
2. Pull up heavy

Sunspot

Sunspots are celestial wars
Concentrated temporary phenomena where
Pores of the glowering photosphere dip dark
In moments of opposite magnetic polarity
Freckles on the hungry not-surface spit rhetoric of
Covert expansion and contraction of garnet euphoria
The Sun covets the Moon and her reign over the tides and the dark
Before the eventual wither and fluttering decay of the crimson blackhead
Time is seized with a sharp blow to the head and
A ray soaked in chloroform
Every atom ceases to vibrate and forms a solid block
Capturing life and death like a negative image on a glass plate

CELIA

She hung floral sheets over the mirrors
When company came, she'd say it was for an art project for the farmer's market
    Or a photoshoot for one of the neighbor girls
    Or because a sheet so pretty deserved to be somewhere more respectable than stretched thin across a ratty old mattress
Plus the bed was where she lost Willie
    And Sam
    And Prudence
A sheet like that didn't need to be sullied with any stains of blood or loss
Celia never dilly dallied and always made sure all the doors and windows were shut before leaving the house for book club
    Or the grocery store
When she got back, she wound her hair up in curlers like noodles on a fork
    And laid out on the veranda smoking her menthol cigarettes
    And humming along to the cicadas
Nothing left of her but a silhouette against Venetian blinds
She smoothed the sheets over the mirrors making sure everything was settled before the Moon rose
    Blinked twice before touching any doorknobs
    Draped hemlock over the banister
    And chewed all her food thirty-six times before swallowing claiming it helped with indigestion and pesky spirits
As long as Celia was around, everyone was safe

The Fisherman

He woke up on a boat
A sliver in the water
The otters knew
The science of dreaming
Even though he had forgotten
He watched the cold Moon
Asked for forgiveness
The stars tied his feet together
Then his body
Until he looked like a pile
Of silver Easter grass
The Moon threw him overboard
Wished him well
I don't want to forget
Yes you do

Aromatherapy

Today the bread sat flat on
The marble cutting board
With a terrycloth rag on top
The kitchen smelled warm
The way you always liked it
And I thought of this day
A year ago or maybe two
When we went to the big city
And ate hot pretzels in the park
How we rode the scooters
On the streets at night in the rain
How I hurt in a way
I couldn't articulate to you
How I cried in the hotel room
And you wouldn't hold me

Hawaiian Night

Stop the car
We are alive
Even if no one else is right now
We'll catch the sunrise
Hide the urgent fuchsia
Behind our eyes
For tomorrow
If things get bad
We'll save the sound of it
Your voice unspooling
Across the ocean
Meeting the whales in
Their breeding ground
I'll snap the hour hand off the sun
Bury it in broken glass
Let it rot in the Texaco parking lot
We only have 3 windows
And tomorrow is today
And we are alive

Ice Cream Saturdae
For Will

Outside the law office on a wooden bench
The plaque reads *Anyone can sit here*
It's kitschy but hey, the town needs it
We are sunburned and barefoot eating ice cream
Butterrumple Butter Pecan and Double Dinosaur Surprise
We toss cone crumbs on the sidewalk
(We wouldn't have if they were waffle cones
Those are 75 cents extra but worth it)
Maybe the birds will eat them when we leave
Or the fat cat that's always slinking about
The Farmer's Elevator across the street
Is always home to a real motley bunch
Of creatures and vermin that come out at night
Too busy thinking about the ecosystem
We're supporting we almost miss
A fancy couple arm in arm walk past
Sunglasses and stilettos on a Saturday
They're definitely not townies
The bell of the law office sounds a flat jingle
Before the door shuts we pretend they ask
Do you guys take walk-in divorces?
Our ice cream is melting quick and
Running like a refrigerator onto our naked feet

The Angle of Eternity

I cannonballed with that penny into the fountain
when I wished that you would change your mind

We met at a midnight grocery store buying a Kit Kat
I wasn't wearing a bra or looking for love

You had kissed the inner corners of my eyes and
asked if I knew what angle eternity traveled at

I tell myself if I had known the answer our love
would've been enough and our happiness infinite

Lost Thing

There's something missing and
I can't seem to find it or
Even remember what it is
I'm looking for
I ransack my room overturning
Papers and untangling necklaces
My bobby pins line the dresser
Like a trail of wiry ants
All in their proper place
The books I'm reading
Are stacked squarely on my bedside table
Next to a couple empty water bottles
Someone told me once that
Catholics pray to a certain saint
When something is lost
But I'm not Catholic
And I can't recall his name

Gera
For my host mother

Gera's father was like Humpty Dumpty when the sickness settled into his bones. It chipped away slowly starting in that place behind his ears that always smelled like cigars. Moments spent idle in his favorite chair in that old farmhouse were miserable. So instead, every Sunday after dinner he stood up from the dining room table, kissed the top of his daughter's head, mounted his horse, and galloped to the beach. Her twin brothers laughed and pointed as their creaky father with the hollow bones rode away.

Her mother was fierce but gentle. She had a sheep on the farm that was born with a defect. Her delicate forearms wrestled it into the world. Everyone told her she would be better off without it, but she refused. One day it broke through the rusty fence knocking down posts and wire and snuffled into the kitchen where she was arms deep in dirty dishes. *Get that damned thing out of our house*, Gera's brothers demanded angrily emphasizing each word with a snap of the towel to the animal's hide.

It was an uncharacteristically sunny day during the rainy season when the twins decided to sell the land. They picked Gera up in their 1985 Hyundai Sonata and putzed their way up the gravel road. She watched as they dug their nails into planks of wood crisscrossed by termites and sunk the heels of their boots into the earth. Papí's favorite chair was too rotted through to salvage. They told her the land was no longer of any value to them. Their parents' passing was long ago, and they needed fast cash.

She argued the farm was more than weathered buildings and trodden ground; it was land locked in time. It was where she had learned how to knead out Abuela's famous tortillas with Mamí looking over her shoulder and dusting flour from her hair. It was where she had learned how to tend to a farm with the kind eyes and sharp wit of their father. It was where she had fallen in love. Her brothers laughed, slapped each other on the back, and shook their heads. *We didn't bring you here for your opinion. We already sold it.*

Gera was six years old when her brothers were born. Up until then, she was the only child on the farm. In the fuzzy hospital sunlight, she climbed atop the thin sweaty mattress her mother lay on and peeked at the two matching bundles. She pushed back their tiny blankets, looked up at her mother with brown sugar eyes and said *that was a lot of work for something so ugly.*

ENTOMOLOGY

Instinct governs that
Moths will always swing drunkenly
Toward flames

Killing themselves in the process
Littering exoskeletons
At the bottom of lanterns

Loving the light so completely
That death by any other means
Could never bear such sweetness

Meanwhile the fireflies
Hide beneath rhubarb leaves
Humming along to the cricket choir

Watching the moths worship the flames
Laughing at their failure
To become the light itself

THE BIG BAY WINDOW

watches the girl who is prodigal of love
sit with knees knitted up under
grandma's patchwork quilt and
a lukewarm mug of chamomile
woven into her palms like a
cylinder of light and gasoline

holds her as she curls into the sill
and presses her fingers into
the meat of an orange
tearing the flesh along the pulpy
seam and smiles remembering
that in spanish the word for
soulmate translates to
media naranja which literally means
half an orange

listens as she hums *la vie en rose*
and decides today is not the day
to write her goodbyes

It's Only Rain

Going For A Walk To Trick Your Brain Into Thinking It's Not Actually Depressed

This is a cool fun trick that only works sometimes
                You can cry during your walks it's okay
The people you pass with their dogs in sweaters   won't notice
They'll just laugh as their dogs take a shit next to a bunch of
        mushrooms growing on
                that old log
And you'll pretend to laugh in your head too
                                Ha ha ha
Because that's what normal people think when they see something funny
When you've finished crying that means it's time for   phase 2
Now you can rehash all the things you feel guilty
        and insecure about
                all day long but can't worry about because you're at work
and there's just too
        much to do
When you've really beaten the dead horse, that's when
                        the magic starts to happen
Your brain goes
            numb and you just concentrate on
                    not stepping on the cracks in the sidewalks
    ****This whole numbwalking thing is **VERY VERSATILE******
You can do it in grocery stores
        YMCAs
             parking lots   anywhere you need to go to get away
If you can convince that middle-aged woman at Planet Fitness that you
        don't in fact need any help finding the elliptical machine and
                that you're doing
                                Just Fine ™
    then maybe you can convince yourself too

Tonight You

Mouth full of wind chimes
Under scuffed sheets of
Eelgrass and toadstools
Grapple and tug with
Hands like soapstone
Nails like granite
Tonight I
Fingers of doubt
Atop knotted redwoods
Spread flat spread thin
Over muscled boulders
Voice like milkweed
Voice like delirium
Voice like wanting

Sirens

He said negativity was for schmucks
Threw his cigars into the fire pit
Never washed his hands

In September he took Elaine to a concert
Sprayed the cats with the hose
Sprayed the neighbor kids with the hose

I learned to skateboard
Skinned my knee twice
Never asked for Band-Aids

Tuesdays sounded like jazz music
Did you know the guy that killed himself?
Yes, I heard the sirens

Blueprint

The blueprint we laid out
In August for forever
Didn't account for

The long sleeve
Of infidelity
Or the humid breath

Of disappointment
Instead it charted
Courses through

Hand holding and nose
Kissing and forgiving
Easy even when it

Never would be
I found the blueprint
Near the waste basket

Under my desk last night
It was a wrinkled ball
And I'd missed

The shot in my
Frustration to rid
Myself of it

Today

I built a red alarm clock
Glittering and tiny
To wind our days around
Pixelated insecurities
Hide behind the backs
Of its skinny hands
If I look at it
It's always today
I wept on the stairs
And knocked it over
The small gadget tumbled
Over the handrail
And landed face first in
The potted plant
You pointed and laughed at it
Kissed my fingertips
Said don't worry
It's tomorrow somewhere

ONCE UPON THIS MORNING

My eyes drifted out of my eyes above violet
raindrops to the slow scrubbing windshield
wipers of the car across the intersection whose
driver I knew in profile who just may be my old
boss from my job before this one but the light
turned to green and the horn behind me pulled
my eyes back into focus and the driver across
the intersection looked forward and I noticed the
hair was different and it wasn't who I thought it
was

Second Summer Without You

You'll be happy to know
James lost his eye
Called it the loveliest egg yolk

Cursed your name
As soon as it was over
Said it was all your fault

Dell got into whittling again
Nicked his finger
Used the red for the gardenias

I gave him modeling clay
And a tube of lipstick
Told him art doesn't have to hurt

Em got into an argument
With a peach pit
Told it to go to hell

I hid it in the dollhouse
Under the miniature staircase
Probably should've just tossed it

Sometimes I read under the trellis
The one you built last summer
All vines and thirst

It's loud outside and in
I'm the only one who can hear it
Addy said I must be crazy

But I know you can hear it too

Blink-182's All The Small Things

I lost 20 pounds and a fistful of hair
Strung it up with periwinkle fishing line
Watched it wave like a flag in traffic
Off the back of your Harley
I wasn't riding with you
Left my helmet on the
Coatrack shaped like a banana
Said I'd meet you there
Might be a little late if I
Messed up the wings of my eyeliner
But while I was getting ready
Singing loud and off-key
I forgot what I was getting ready for
And decided to take a nap instead

Winter Road Trip

We drove across the state
In the middle of a night blizzard
Angry at each other
Your left hand snow white
On the steering wheel
You lost the other glove
Tires fumbling and losing traction
On ice frozen over a crust of salt
The heat in your car had been
Broken for months
My parka and jeans too thin
Like cobwebs in morning frost
We can pull off here and
Wait for the snow to let up
But you kept your foot on the gas
Even though we couldn't see through
Flurries a foot ahead of us
The fat flakes in the headlights
Felt like we were driving through stars
You icicle tongue
Me frostbitten breath
The car a box of arctic silence

NYC Noon
For Theda

I couldn't write yesterday
Too busy worrying about you
So small
In a big city
Were you being safe
On the subways
Not talking to strangers
Not getting too chummy
With old men in bodegas
Drinking enough water
I hope
And always running
Demanding your place
Tearing up the streets
Toppling buildings
And shitty Uber drivers
With steel-toed dreams
And your mother's charm

Fever Dream

I break the length of my braids
On copper wires and candy floss
All before breakfast

Kicking and screaming down snow globe
Stairs to a mirror maze kitchen
All the cupboards are open

Tarantula Jenny touches a
Honeycomb cheek
Not my honeycomb cheek

Gran has peanut butter skin
Irons her fever into ribbons
The rabbit-eared TV is upside down

Snake Lady fills another jar
Dances on the orange bowl of the sunset
I don't recognize anyone in the photographs

WRITER'S BLOCK

When I try to write but
The words lie comatose
I default to thinking of you and
That spot I like on your forearm
To provide spasmodic inspiration
But I'm running out of you
The same way I'm running out of words

On the Edge of 84th Street

Lives a big maple tree
Knotted roots bisecting
The northernmost perimeter
Of someone's front yard
It's grown broad and tall
And its branches reach
Higher than the chimney

When the telephone wires
Got in the way of its
Photosynthetic grandeur
The road commission
In high-vis and hard hats
Set up orange signs
Took chainsaws and
Hacked a big L into the wood
Allowing the wire to
Pass through unobstructed

Now it extends its arms in
Arabesque as if it had never
Known any other way to grow

The Goddess Athena
For Mariah

She fell from Zeus' forehead during one of his
migraines – already too powerful to be contained
even by the King of the Gods

Ares educates her on the brutality of construction
paper warfare. At first, she practices on herself.
Papercuts crosshatch her inner thighs.

But she grows wiser. She wipes the blood from
her legs and calmly folds the construction paper
into boats. Ares' sword and spear are no match.

She rumors the boats into fibers and spins them
into five flowers of gold and ivory – the love
languages. She lets Aphrodite take the credit.

The people celebrate her. She offers them a
reprieve from monsters they are too afraid to
face themselves. They erect a city in her name.

On clear nights she lays under her olive tree,
gathers her tunic up about her, and takes seven
deep breaths – one for each drop of blood spilt.

As the Moon rises to carouse with the stars, she
lets her eyes close. The wind traces her scars.
She is not in need of a hero. She just needs to rest.

Dust Bunny Daydream

The light
Underneath the clavicle
The one tucked beneath
The coil of the bed spring
Feathery and prismatic
Burnt out a while ago
Now it rattles
Like an old lightbulb
And no one ever came by
To change it

Waiting

An older man on a bicycle trundles by with an arm full of wet newspapers. The ink smears and runs onto the sleeves of his jacket. He skids over the cobbles. The tail of water sputtering after him splashes the tips of my sneakers.

We wait for the bus clumped under the terracotta roof of El Sagrario. Our fists are teacups for the rain. The air is thick and quiet and sleepy. The group is worn, but we know the bus will at least have air conditioning.

A young couple crosses the street without noticing the small group of bedraggled tourists. Her butterfly lips skim the stubble of his cheek. She runs ahead of him. He threads his way between parked cars to follow her lightning laugh.

I peel off my socks and shoes. You watched me peel off my jeans the night before in pale yellow light and twisted iron bars and a hand stitched quilt. One foot in the cool puddle. One foot on the rough gravel. Take my hand. It's only rain.

Communing With The Moon

I dipped my fingers in the Moon
And she said it was *soda* not *pop*
She twirled her snowbranch braids
Like glittering nunchucks
My body disappeared up to my eyes
Her voice was the color of a peppermint mist
I told her my first memory
She told me not to stop for pebbles in my shoe

In The Mountains

Pomegranate sun hung heavy by a celestial Command Hook / boots on boulders / swollen hands swinging / wiping brows / uncapping water bottles / pocketing stone souvenirs / initials carved in moon bleached bark / M + J 4EVR / more like 5 months / this was the day we ate PB&Js in a rental car / altitude drenched dizziness / toes icy in Emerald Lake / we laugh in the photos / but all I remember / is you crying / telling us / how he touched you / that night / how you kept pulling down your shirt / burrowed deeper in woolen blankets / but / he / would / not / stop /

On The Deck

There's a hornets' nest
On the top step
Between two
Faded and
Splintered slats
Last year
There was
A robin's nest
With three
Speckled eggs
Peter said
You have to get rid
Of hornets' nests
At night
Because that's when
They sleep
Just like us
But I don't believe him

The Tourist

She appears in the background of photos
rolling a joint out of stories from your lips
making more up out of the chaos she conjures
her celadon eyes aren't hers

After dinner she might stay for game night
finger brushing over dusty bookshelves
you tell her your best college stories
while she weighs your old textbook in her hands

The silver top hat from Monopoly is gone
prisoner in her pocket the next morning
the air has grown too lifeless for her
she was never here for you anyway

Neon Love Song

They lay upside down
Four feet stacked on top of each other
Building a Jenga tower with Motel 6 pillows
Bodies slick with the patina of love
He tasted like a game of truth or dare
And she never knew which
Was more delicious

REM

Tiny old babies dripping wet
Plump bodies in the kitchen sink
Our hair perfect sudsy sprouts
Together we are stuck
Backwards blistered loving
Fat faces smushed with oatmeal
Laughs inside out when you
Ride your bike into the street
Halloween will be different
This time around and don't forget curfew
Tongue kissing on the ceiling and
Comforters on the roof
Only grown-ups allowed in the tree house
Dad said maple leaves make good knives
Yours is under the rock in the garden
My phone charges on my pillow
Just in case you call
I sleepwalk under the counter
When you find me I'm 100 years old
My feet have grown into the wood grain
Of the table and chairs
You have to use the red chainsaw
To cut me loose

Stay

Stop the train
And the bus
And all the cars in the world
The planes can fly
But only if they go backwards
Today is for stop
Tomorrow can be go
Breathe in and out
Slowly
Fold the time zones over
Into paper cranes
Today is for you
Shouldn't be
But I don't make the rules
Lay with me
Sweet quiet low

(This poem begins and ends with text excerpted from The God of Small Things *by Arundhati Roy)*

A LOVE LETTER TO MY GOD OF SMALL THINGS

He folded his fear into a perfect rose. He held it out in the palm of his hand. She took it from him and put it in her hair.

Lay me down and split me open like a frog on a dissecting table. Kiss the bruises your hip bones left on my inner thighs. You can have my cannibal nightmares if you want. I'm not that scared anymore.

Let me taste the fingers that poured too much cinnamon. I bet they still taste sweet. I'll punch confetti out of your notebooks and sprinkle leaves I found near the bus stop in their place. You don't have to pick up the pieces.

You can have the crickets I caught in second grade and the crescent scar on my elbow. But I know you won't want lunch tomorrow. I'll take the night you taught me about the universe expanding and the Polaroid in your wallet.

Whisper upside down secrets into the neckplace behind my ear. The one that you kissed last month. Give me your hand in kaleidoscope darkness and the way you touch when you want to tell me something but don't know how.

I have loved you this long. I will be okay.

The Big Things ever lurked inside. They knew that there was nowhere for them to go. They had nothing. No future. So they stuck to the small Things.

To My Birth Mother

Voicemail 6:47 PM: Hi Mom! Or do you prefer "Mother"? It's all kind of abstract, isn't it? Haha. I just wanted to give you a call to thank you for giving me my best chance. I was at work today (I'm a waitress!) and a customer grabbed my ass as I was walking back to the kitchen. People are always saying to ignore things like that because you'll get farther in life if you do, but it awakens a dragon in my belly. Did I get that from you? My sister had a baby two years ago and I've watched her grow into her nose (my sister's nose) and her chin (her dad's chin), and it makes me wonder who I look like most. Did I get my long piano fingers from you or Dad? Who did I get my stuttering tin can kneecaps from? My body always wants to be held, but maybe that's because my family doesn't really touch, and you didn't hold me too long. It's okay. I forgive you for that. When I graduated from college last year (summa cum laude!), I wished you were there to see me. I think you'd be really proud.

The First Snow of The Year

Always comes as a surprise
Partly because I never check the radar
Partly because I don't want to think about
Icicle fingers sealing the sides of windows
Morning frost like nubby sheets
Black ice pinging cars back and forth

The first flakes in the chilled air
Catch me off guard again this November
Partly because our Christmas tree isn't up yet
Partly because I put the wrong shoes on this morning
And my ankles are already turning blue

To Someone But I Can't Remember Who

Marry me inside a paper lantern
Our parents don't have to be there
A praying mantis can officiate
Your side of the aisle will be past lovers
Mine will be future ones
Everyone will sit on pearl thimbles
We can stay trapped in our honeymoon mason jar
Wear whatever you want
I'll make sure winters are cozy
As long as you keep reading to me
When you cut yourself on the glass
I'll embroider it all better blindfolded
You always liked my art because of the way
It made you ache

Growth (Or Lack Thereof)

Anxiety Metaphors II

My dresser is full
The sock drawer won't close
And the bottom of the pajama drawer
Sags like a smile

I never learned how to pick locks
Even though Dad could teach me
I was never any good
At remembering my keys

On Tuesdays my bed folds around
The shell of my body
Forgotten in an afternoon nap
I dream I can bend spoons with my mind

Otters hold each other's paws
To keep from floating apart
I saw one at the zoo cradle a fish
Before shredding its head with its teeth

TRAVERSE CITY BUSINESS TRIP

we saw a snake in the leaves / he wore his hood up high around his head / *like your sister* / mom joked / she told us to stay still / wait for him to go back / beth & margot slept on the second floor / well not really / a little nook halfway up the stairs / stevie & i got the basement / mom & dad the main floor / the condo owner crammed the beds / like tetris pieces / *not a business trip ... a business vacation* / the night was fine / dull & gray & languorous / we were right on the lake / i dreamt i was drowning / someone knocked at 2 in the morning / stevie threw her sock at me / *wake up* / she hissed like that snake / dad hobbled to the door / groggy & naked / except for his red fruit of the loom briefs / we watched from the crack of the kitchen door / *sorry ... no phillip here ... wrong condo* / we stayed still / waited for him to go back

BRUISED EGO

I slipped on the ice
In the parking lot
On the way into
The doctor's office
I fell a little
Before catching
My balance
And the concrete
Hump of the curb
Met my ankle
Now I have a
Plum colored bruise
The size of a quarter
It hurts only a little less
Than seeing you
Without me

Obit

Symbiosis passed away peacefully January 31, 2021. We let it snuffle and gasp for air before holding the pillow over its face. We agreed it was for the best. You still have scratches on your forearms. I watched a documentary about coral reefs. When the water becomes too warm, the coral evicts all the algae living within its walls causing it to lose its color. The reefs become Gaudí-inspired structures of bone and lace. None of this has been your fault. Sharing became a burden too great for either of our tired backs. Life spliced us apart like a pair of conjoined twins. It would be impossible to count all the times I let you down on only two hands. But you could have at least shown up for the funeral.

EMERGENCY NOTICE

There are bombs out there
Ripe like peaches
But you have to be careful
The pits can be tricky
Be up on time every day
And make sure your sister
Eats all her lunch
Stay away from the light
And the crowds
The dark is safer
Don't worry about us
Or the paper houses
You'll be better off here
Away from the peaches
Away from us

Bodega Baby

The traffic lights delight themselves
In the way you taste

Like fireworks and old perfume
The halcyon New York City of movies

You lost your two front teeth early
Smashed your pretty face

On a bench in Central Park
Tripping over your pink Velcro sneakers

Everything tasted like static for a week
The bodega cat laughed

Mermaid Caves

Take me raindrop lover
Into the old cavern
Where veins of
Untouched minerals
Crack themselves open
For us and unfold me
Like a bolt of lace
Down from the
Stalactites we are
Nothing but
Silkworms and
Bioluminescence
Unfurl secrets
Long buried in
Bone boxes that the
Earth will never tell

(This poem was inspired by Cannibal Woman *by Ada Limón)*

MASOCHISTIC HEROINE

I read a poem about a poem
About a mosquito woman
Eating away at all that she knew
The ground beneath her scorched with
The remains of lovers and friends

> *Aristotelian characters*
> *The famed tragic heroes*

She started out as a cannibal
As we all do
With feet like thunder
And breath like eternity

> *Met their demise because of*
> *Their fatal flaw*

But her hunger was too deep
Her anger too raw
The ash fell like silk rain as
She became her own destruction

> *What's known as their hamartia*

But unlike the fabled valiant heroes
She craved the ruin
It hummed like rose water on her skin

Sunnyfield Ave

At the end of the road
There's a street lamp
That never goes out
I've seen every other one
Serviced by maintenance
Over the years
But not this one
All of the lamps cast
LED halos like a
String of bluish pearls
Frosting the barren street
Every night at 7
But this one is still yellow

GROWTH (OR LACK THEREOF)

I wish I could write about
How I climbed a mountain

After falling into a pit of depression
And emerged a new woman

But the truth is I didn't and
I'm not haunted by the hike

And its scenery and the sweat
As we fumbled down the rocky gorge

I said I was considering lash extensions
But I rub my eyes too much

And M thought I said
I love my eyes too much

She told me she had been waiting
So long to see me love myself

I didn't have the heart to tell her
I don't yet

A Lesson in Vocabulary and Anatomy

Aubergine is another word for eggplant
I can't tell if I like it but I think you do
Your mouth opens and closes around it
Like a locked secret *oh brr sheen*
It sounds like pebbles in a microwave
After dinner you can teach me anatomy
Undress me slowly and label all my bones
Show me where my hyoid floats
Tell me another secret hidden between your lips
Satsuma is a type of orange
The word wreaths my hair like lavender
Your voice rough on my neck *sat soo ma*

Summer

Bare elbows on the hood of the car
Bumblebees mistake my hair for home

Deaf eye looked left saw checkerberries blush
Did it see the calico cat yawn?

Money crumpled twisted
Moping but smiling shiny like nickels

Slate gray storm clouds
Sentimental white lichen on the rocks

My lips my right breast
Muskmelon-stained teeth

Dimpled cheeks spat seeds
Dared the cornflowers to bow

Bellies helpless and warm
Believe me when I cross my heart

After Hours

We drank wine on the patio under the thin blinking stars. S ordered pizza and we listened to Selena's Cómo la flor. H touched L's cheek. They worked together for years, but didn't fall in love until he asked what she was reading in the break room one day. I'll be home late tonight; don't wait up. I can't wait to tell you all about it in the morning. The patio furniture scraped the concrete as H pulled L into his arms laughing. Listen, Neruda's poetry is garbage, he called out to me. Heat lightning flashed in the distance. I imagine the thunder like Sunday church bells. There wasn't much space to move. They danced anyway. S brought out more drinks. Tomorrow is her daughter's birthday. Unfortunately, she'll be spending it with her ex-husband. Her drink limit is 4, but who's counting? We finished our work early, and it was a Friday night. Sangria fell from her glass. Good thing she was already wearing red. So, tell me about your boyfriend! To tell you the truth, I would rather dance.

Little Bennie Franklin

Thought she could be forever
With birthday candle teeth and
A pocket full of keys in the thunderstorm
But when she felt the cold air
And the night mist
Falling like dominoes
She ran all the way home

(This poem begins with text excerpted from Love in the Time of Cholera *by Gabriel García Márquez translated by Edith Grossman)*

HURACÁN FERMINA

Florentino Ariza hung the mirror in his house, not for the exquisite frame but because of the place inside that for two hours had been occupied by her beloved reflection

Hurricane legs unfolded
Creamy center
Stone bridges bent
Their backs in the
Eye socket of the storm
The mirror struck him
Across the face
Fingers white on the frame
Spinning wildly up and out
Body wrapped around
Trembling in the tempest
The eye of the storm
Should be still like ending
But he clung desperately
Chocolate blood on the gold paint
Invaluable and cushioned
Protected by his weight
Arms wouldn't let go
For a fleeting moment
He held her reflection like
Venus in a lapis clamshell

Adrift

Binge-loving you
Didn't blind me this time
The wind left my sails slowly
And I coasted on the gray sea
I didn't scrape the barnacles off the hull
Or pretend I was some great sailor
I didn't need to
This time you climbed aboard
All on your own
Asked if I saved you a seat
And we bobbed on the water
Watching the still ocean
I made myself quiet
Folded in like a telescope
Because that's what you needed
We read Life of Pi
Argued whether everyone died
Slaughtering each other to survive
Or if they were animals all along
We both knew we might
Never find land
And if worse came to worst
I never learned how to swim

Allison

Allison said
Everything is purple

And she twisted
Wild indigo into the bookshelves

Told Noah
To stop crying at night

And took her medicine
With a glass of lilac wine

The Tin Man

He was a robot built with the wrong pieces
All elbows and shoulders and nuts and bolts
A mass of metal and skin and frayed wires
But his manufacturers made a mistake
They gave him a heart of pulsating flesh and blood
And when the vibrations of her whisper rattled through
He was a pinball machine all lit up

His fear and love produced a cloud of spun caramel
A yellow nest for her to put her loose change and her youth
But they were lost before they could be found
And all that stood were brittle sugared strands
A sicksweet smell of an old friend's blanket
Rust under fingernails like orange Velcro
And a secret passed in paper shadows

She reached for the self-destruct button

The Tree Sprite Stopped Asking Riddles At The Bridge - She Wasn't A Troll After All
For Sydney

She grew tired of it. The passersby were far too obtuse to ever truly know the answers anyway.

Now she is fearless in her probing. She can unearth buried treasure tied up in your ribcage.

But she is never cruel. She is patient. If you come early enough, she'll fix you avocado toast.

Sometimes the lines on her map change. She doesn't mind. Her compass always points north.

Two Hands

Rest easy together
An accordion of platonic prayer
Across freckled shins
I spilled milk tea on the bed sheets
When you weren't looking
Will you grab a trash bag
While you're out?
I want to toss my feelings
Somewhere appropriate
For the night

Norman Rockwell's *Freedom From Want*

She can cut that last grapefruit into thirds
One for Mom and one for Dad and one for Grace
I'll julienne the carrots and cry in the bathroom
Before dinner make sure there are fresh flowers in the vase
Mom likes yellow but that color makes Simon anxious
He covered the floor with thumbtacks like rows of candy soldiers before we tore down the wallpaper
Dad won't be able to hear Twyla over the sunset
She'll just have to talk prettier
If there are any insects making frenzied love in the salad bowl, would you kindly excuse yourselves?
We're trying to have a nice family dinner here
Amber can't stand the sight of that tablecloth and I can't say I blame her
Plastic toadstools remind us of the pediatrician with the rattail
When there's only one buttered roll left Mom and Dad can split it like usual
Merle made pistachio ice cream for dessert
Dad snuck a Milky Way out of his sleeve
Tell them I'll be out in just a minute

A Lesson in Self-Sufficiency

I pulled my heart out
Through my ribcage
It opened like a set of elevator doors
And hummed like a six-cylinder engine
I wrapped it carefully
In banana leaves
And let it dry in the sun
The sea breeze lifted
Edges of the parcel
But the unbearable weight
Kept it tight to the earth
Tomorrow I'll cut it in two
And mail half to your apartment
If you forget to return it
When you're done
Don't worry
I'll find a way to get it back
Just like last time

Daisy

Daisy was six years old when the Apollo 11 landed on the Moon. The stars were plucked from their place in the sky like cotton balls and brought back for all Americans to have as nightlights. Her father with big brick laying hands lifted her high onto his shoulders and told her to count the stars. *When you finish counting, know that that's how much I love you.*

Daisy was forty-nine when the Curiosity Rover landed on Mars. Her father watched Channel 8 on the small screen in the hospital room and wondered if a robot could feel lonely stranded among all those stars. His big brick laying hands were not as strong anymore, but they held hers over the cold plastic of the bed's railing. His breath was light like a skipping stone. *Have you finished counting yet?*

Not even close.

The Harvest

She fancied herself a bit of a goddess
Nothing special
Not a despot like Zeus or a disgruntled wife like Hera
Just someone who revels in Dionysian exploits from time to time
On Thursdays she met with J
Always at 11 sharp for cocktails
In bed she told him about the others
Lovers her ruthlessness didn't bother sparing
Men whose eyeballs she harvested
To drop like olives in her martinis
J never believed her
He kissed her neck
How could anyone ever stop looking at you?
She dug trenches into the headboard with her fingernails
As his breath shallowed in sleep
Opening and closing like a moth's soft wings
The breeze from the window lifted the sheets
His body shivered before turning over
She counted the freckles on his back
Stood up carefully so as not to wake him
And topped off a glass of gin

If You Find Me Again

You might not recognize me
My nose is the same
And the shoulders you loved into five different cities
But my hair is a little bit longer
And my laugh is round now like all those dumplings we ate last summer

I want you to know I didn't forget
All those notes you left squirreled away for me
Trying to Hansel and Gretel me home when I got lost
I remember you in that red dress
You're the best at beautiful
My sweet love
But you stopped wanting me to come home
And I dreamt of the forest

I hope I recognize you
The same heavygentle hands
And the legs that itch to dance when you've had a couple beers
But I hope you're happier too
Just like me

The Five Stages of Grief

I. Walk outside in the winter in just your socks and underwear. Suck in so much frigid air that your lungs become crystal balls. Try your hand at fortune telling.

II. Pile all your clothes in the middle of the living room. Burrow underneath so only your nose pokes out of the heap. Set them on fire with that candle you never liked the smell of.

III. Watch the ants coming out of the crack in the sidewalk. Give them the rest of your bagel. Apologize for burning them with a magnifying glass when you were six with your cousin.

IV. Ask your mom to tell you about her honeymoon. Pretend you can hear the rain on the roof of their cabin in Montauk. Pretend you can imagine them in love.

V. Take a pottery class or two. Collapse your vase like a tire on the highway. Admit you like the collapse more than the vase. Do it again. Smile. Finally.

www.ingramcontent.com/pod-product-compliance
Lightning Source LLC
Chambersburg PA
CBHW022113090426
42743CB00008B/833